Bare Hands

Bare Hands

Poems

Lindsey Royce

Turning Point

[signature] 2016

Dear Joan,
Thanks for your
support of my work
at Brooklyn College.
Grateful —
Fondly,
Lindsey

Published by Turning Point
P.O. Box 541106
Cincinnati, OH 45254-1106

ISBN: 978-1-62549-205-0

Poetry Editor: Kevin Walzer
Business Editor: Lori Jareo

Visit us on the web at www.turningpointbooks.com.

Cover design: Tattoo design by Eric Edelman, Art of
    RetroCollage, New York, New York, and Melissa
    Freeman, Deluxe Tattoo, Steamboat Springs, Colorado

Cover photograph: Cyndi Marlowe, Steamboat Springs,
    Colorado

Author photo: Cyndi Marlowe,
    www.cyndimarlowephotography.com

for

Wendy Baumann & Harriet Elkington

Man is a god in ruins . . . Infancy is the perpetual Messiah, which comes into the arms of fallen men, and pleads with them to return to paradise.

—Ralph Waldo Emerson

You see, when weaving a blanket, an Indian woman leaves a flaw in the weaving of that blanket to let the soul out.

—Martha Graham

Someone I loved once gave me a box full of darkness.

It took me years to understand that this, too, was a gift.

—Mary Oliver

Acknowledgments

Thanks to the editors of the journals in which the following poems appeared, some in different versions:

Amelia: "My Father's Heart"
Calliope: "The Little Engine that Could" and "The Repair"
Cutthroat: "Swallowing It" and "My Mother's Wallpaper"
Empty Sink Publishing: "Call Center for Madonna/Whore Support" and "Watching Her Neigh"
Maryland Poetry Review: "Burden of Proof" (published as "Proof Positive")
MockingHeart Review: "Last Things"
Mudfish: "The Fatherly Season" (published as "Father's Choice")
New York Quarterly: "The Art of Shape" (published as "Style")
Poet Lore: "Polished"
Switched-on Gutenberg: "Photo of My Father at Twelve"
Washington Square: "My Father the Bard"

Sincere thanks to the following people who commented on these poems in various stages of development: Doug Anderson, Roberta Feins, Scott Hightower, Molly Peacock, and Pam Uschuk. Also, warm thanks to Kathryn Peterson and other friends and colleagues who provided encouragement in the revision process. Finally, gratitude to my publishers, Kevin Walzer and Lori Jareo, for believing in this collection.

Contents

I

The Fatherly Season

From a distance, I watch my father raking,
belt bent beneath the weight of his gut,
wingtips he hits me with matting tracks in damp
grass, trip-spring mouth cursing twigs that snare
the rake. Sometimes, my father sweeps leaves for me,
and I dash across the lawn: streak of Injun braids
and feathers, airplane speeding on a runway,
cannonball, kangaroo, bursting russet-red and gold. Careful
never to dart too close. Careful never to laugh too loud.
So in love—with him, the crisp air, with rare hours
his steely words descending light as leaves.

My Father the Bard

The British say bonk, shag, chat her up. You
chat her up so you can bonk her. My father
is delighted. *Princess Diana is bonking him,*
but he's shagging the other broad. Bonk, bonked,
has bonked. Shag, shagged, is shagging.
The Irish call it fecking or getting into your gowl.
Feck off, feck out, feck up, feck up up and away—

A dexterous reviler, he worked his sounds well,
hitting with iambs, maybe a spondee to wind up:
Cocksucking motherfucking dizzy little bastard.
Shut your fag hole, you mollycoddled can of piss.
No loving words for his namesake, who'd run to the arms of trees.
While I hid in our fort, my father's words broke branches like fists.

Mom was *keg legs, bitty titties, battle-axe bitch,*
alliteration that cracked whips to strike and strip her
of her dignity. When I wasn't cut by his words,
I was dazzled by their power to make her rage
and cry as she smashed commemorative ashtrays
over my father's feet. And though I rooted for his head,
and Lincoln came close, she settled for his knees.

Nothing helped the void inside when he called me *cunt,*
slut, whore, slapper, scrubber, words that etched blue
tattoos even though I didn't know their meanings.
He fumed at *Eleanor of Abington,* who would *gallivant*
and *piss away money* with friends, while he was stuck
at a desk in a *government shithole,* buying
airplane parts for those who had adventures.

Worse, he would phone her all day to get an endless ring,
fearing she'd flown abroad, left him for the handsome dentist
who wanted to spirit her away to Paris or Venice,

despite Dad's best cadenced hate, words thrown to cripple
yet compelling alive—and worlds away
from everyday speech in pattern, variation. My ear
wholly open for collisions of sound—*stupid git, brazen
brat, effin' eejit, omadhan*—his demand that we listen up,

choke down his filth, his *droich-chaint* digging
graves for us. Did he know his crude rhythms
would one day forge the spade
I would use to dig my song free?

The Self-made Man

Picking her up for that first date shocks you.
The foyer's chandelier, you learn, is cleaned with gin,
Chippendale cushions so white you fret if your trousers
are clean. When my not-yet-mother descends the stairs,
is she as charming as her self-made father?

A silver service is set before you; tea poured,
your fingers, clumsy. You fear you'll nick the china
on your teeth, a far sight from the row home
you grew up in: rough borough, Irish immigrant parents
so poor the knockoff Victorian sofa is threadbare,

and the deer on your wall with dead glass eyes
can't help you foresee how her father's gifts will curdle
your soul—starter house in the suburbs, summer home by the sea,
cars, stocks, the Windsor rocker I cower behind, its slatted
back like prison bars against the shouting and smashing glass.

My Father's Animals

My dad's dog, Woodrow, is a biter, hence my dad jokes about Woodrow's temper, nicknames him *Hellion* and hell's compounds—*Hellmouth, Hellfire, Hellhound, Hellacious Whelp from Hell*. He also baby talks to crabby old Woodrow: *Woody, do you have a woody? How's the wood hangin', old man? Woody, you want Mother to take care of your morning wood?*

His cockatiel, Freshie, drew blood from everyone but him. Then, Dad bought PeePee, the duck, which he called Shitpot, because PeePee pooped in Mom's pot of soup and kept *her* flying around the house cleaning creamed-spinach droppings off furniture and rugs. And if soup wasn't enough, once PeePee landed one in Mom's Victrola on Bing Crosby's album, *El Señor Bing*. The shit spun until Bing's voice distorted on a chorus. Olé.

No more birds, Mom said. So Dad brought several dozen eggs home for Easter. He kept them on his workbench under an incubator, saying he wanted them for stew or shish kebab, and my young self pictured him skewering a series of newborn chicks with green peppers and onions. Maybe a cherry tomato. At the image of impaled chicks chirping and squirming on the skewer, I cried, *Please give them to Jesus on Easter.* But my father said if there were no kebabs, he'd flush the chicks down the toilet.

Before they disappeared, I would watch my father spend hours feeding each one with an eyedropper, cradling each fragile body in the palm of his hand. If one didn't make it through the night, he'd say, *Poor bastard went missing.* My mom, avoiding the garage entirely, wanted nothing to do with the chicks because they were there and because Dad had cut the clean, new undershirts she'd bought with an X-ACTO knife to make soft linings for their boxes. I watched him slash the tees with an anger that made me wonder what kept him from crushing each chick like a paper cup in his hands.

Photo of My Father at Twelve

Sitting on the running board of a neighbor's old Ford,
you have a guarded look in your eyes. At once,
you appear relaxed and tense, bare chest taut,
nipples like buds, skin milky, ribs sticking out.
You want to be a boy with boy's dreams,
though you try on men's rules for size,
and if you could remember a hug or kiss,
a time when nurture wasn't *mollycoddling*,
you'd go back there by magic carpet and rest.
Having learned to be lonely, you hate your need,
your secret longing to be held like your sisters,
and bitter as an orange peel, you've discarded
sweetness as you soldier on—not yet brutal
toward wife and children: it's here I would step
in the frame, lift you, dear child, into my arms,
smooth the furrow from your forehead,
and hug away the grief, the fucked up, wrong.
I'd say, *Boy, your sensitivity isn't weak.*
Sit with me until the trouble leaves, until you trust
again, until your small self grows peaceful,
and even, if we're lucky, radiant with love.

Forbidden Fruit

At ten, I pocketed sugared orange slices at the Penny Candy Store, slipping them in my windbreaker, blue as Mother Mary's robes. To evade police, I rushed up a prayer.

My hand sweaty on the sweets, I fled, Sister Mary Catherine's voice rasping Revelations in my head: *You'll go to hell, the lake that burns with fire and brimstone, the second death . . . You'll never escape!*

Sister Mary Catherine made hell seem akin to the horror film that scarred me the time I snuck out of *The Apple Dumpling Gang* and into *Jaws,* a movie my mother forbade. Sister Mary Catherine seemed to like blood as much as the shark did: When other nuns decorated their classes with white lilies for Easter, Sister Mary Catherine hung Jesus dripping gore from the cross.

There was always confession and absolution. In line with other schoolgirls in the carcass-like church, I'd wait for my turn to kneel and whisper lies to the priest. Cheating and disobeying my parents seemed mild enough sins to admit, yet I sometimes peppered my confession with realism — pantsing my brother, burying his blankie — as I suspected priests perceived plausibility.

* * *

Vicki and I walked the boardwalk, browsing trendy window displays. Back Pockets was the hippest store, its jewelry case stocked with goodies like goddess amulets, knot rings, and puka shell necklaces. Vicki called me to the dressing room and asked if she should steal a bikini, crocheted red.

In a proper confession, the penitent tells the priest all her sins. Omission means no absolution. For years, I'd put off truth, learning confession was a Hail Mary football pass. You had to get honest only once, and you'd score heaven right away. Even if you were luckless and died so fast you couldn't make a last ditch Act of Contrition, you would end up in purgatory, and your surviving relatives could pray you in. Sudden death overtime.

This time, Vicki had to decide for herself. I left the storefront lit by blue and red lights and slowly walked home on the boardwalk, a walk I'd taken hundreds of times past Wonderland Amusements, Brown's Donuts, Dave's Bike Rentals, and last, the Penny Candy Store, where I'd tallied my soul with black marks, licorice coins eclipsing any light that could have helped.

The Pin Oak, the Oracle

Does it hurt to be a nascent leaf
pushed forth from a scar in the bark?
Does it burn to deepen green,
to hold the scalding light to your chest?
Is it painful to bleed into colors,
blaze like a monk in his saffron robe?
When the severance comes and the free fall,
does it hurt with great relief?

II

My Mother's Wallpaper

By eleven, I had hoped to work my mother like a spigot.
My siblings could do so, but I hadn't learned,
so when my father hurled his wingtip at me,
sidearmed like a shortstop firing at first,
I ran to the kitchen to tell Mother what he'd done.

I found her elbow-deep in dishwater,
blurted he had hit me with his shoe,
the swelling on my head like a soft-boiled egg.
But Mom didn't answer, so I said he'd called me
bad names, and that failed, too. So I said,

The shoe scuffed your new white wallpaper.
Gently, my mother rinsed a clean dishtowel
and went to the freezer for ice. Then, she took
the ice pack to the scuff-marked wall, and nursed
that paper for what she thought we were worth.

Polished

Who knew I could stand against anything?
I puzzled over the Black maids
who bussed from city to suburbs to clean,
who knocked at our door, only to be sent to
the basement to change from one ragged
dress and wig to a second, even shabbier set.
I saw those dirty, pink slippers on Bertha's
misshapen feet, which moved glacier slow
across our floors. Stone silent, deliberate
as a gavel, she chewed through half-hour lunches,
bore the bridge club's finger-sandwich voices
disturbing even the air they breathed.
Before the guests, I'd watch Bertha bend
to set the tea stand and silver service buffed enough
to reflect us all, and I'd feel lucky to be white.
Years later, I'd see her brown fingers aging pinkish-
gray, and, fake ID in my back pocket,
I'd overtip Leroy, the bartender, still washing away
what had tarnished my hands.

Country Club Funerals

Early to my grandmom's funeral luncheon,
scanning the banquet room's tables,
I sat lady-still: pressed, white cloths, white
rose centerpieces, bleached, blemish free.
Men in tailored summer suits
lined the ornate, cherry-wood bar,
drinks icing one hand, smokes yellowing
the other; women clucking, settling
children stiff in snowy pinafores
and suits, short pants and knee socks
for the littlest boys. As afternoon light
melted to butter and Black servers
brought drinks on round trays, voices
amped with alcohol. I put on my best
country club self, sipped a Shirley Temple,
checking the room for another heathen
who questioned it all, saw burlesque
in so much privilege, who balked: *Burn my body;*
scatter the ashes somewhere beautiful
or somewhere ugly where I took a stand.

Keepin' It Real

I walked both worlds, pleasant with Mom's White lady-friends, who wore gold chains thick as leashes and doorknob diamonds to the beach, while their husbands downed martinis beside docked boats with names like *Lazy Days* and *Sea Spray*. I was "tight" with Blacks, tho: Queenie of the killer set shot, Ebony, a superior ball handler, and Gayle, who could block most buckets but mine, one thing they respected. The girls gave me honorary status, the nickname "Zippy" for my speed 'cause I'd outrun them, and praise that my fadeaway jump shot was "off the hook."

My mother stressed out over my Black friends, yet palmed me sly cash to go "chillaxin'" after games at Mack's Pizza Joint on the boardwalk—neutral turf—since all the girls' homes were off limits to other races. We'd come together in this no-man's-land, at a Formica table, sharing pizza so good greasy cheese stretched a whole foot to our hunger. We ate. Drank 7-Up. Laughed together. Just people.

Call Center for Madonna/Whore Support

When I dare to sit on a public toilet, where does my mother come from? Some warped synapse in my mind, a sniper firing from one cell to another?

You must paper the seat. Arrange the paper, double-ply, over a pretend softball diamond, home to first and third to home the most essential safeguards. Perch on the seat's edge and avoid the outfield altogether. If any plastic should touch your bottom, you'll get "dirty," "unsanitary," "unclean," then you'll be a loose woman.

Loose women were hard, teeth yellow from nicotine, eyes pleated and brimming with unrequited everything, like the sinners in my artwork gazing up at saintly nuns, all of whom remained as serenely detached as lightbulbs.

Where in Western art are images of female, adult, lay sinners praying to female saints? Or to Mother Mary? Even Magdalene's makeover—body cleanse and career change— doesn't get her prayed to in art. There's some go-getting in *St. Catherine Exorcising the Demon from a Possessed Woman*—but for Catherine, it's no real money shot. You want your female saints to flex big guns, but all you get is them alone (and meek), loafing with other saints (and meek), or being martyred to keep their virginity (still meek, while dying heinous deaths).

So Marla, the only atheist I knew, burst into my first apartment: *I caught the worst case of herpes my doctor's ever seen,* the mess on her "holy of holies" merely inconvenient.

31

And I got it from a one-night stand! Disease, one-night stand, no shame? Wow! How impressive and unique to atheists, I thought. Marla, bitching by my kitchenette: with her big eyes and blonde curls, she looked like a Valentine cherub bred with Bianca Jagger.

When Marla left, the toilet loomed large. I guessed she hadn't papered, and my mind recited a litany of cleaning products:

> Lysol Spray: *kills household germs, including germs that cause odors*
> Clorox Bleach: to bleach or not to bleach. *They all did laundry, maybe even a man . . .*
> Playtex Gloves: medium pink, *superior protection and comfort,* like in their ads for tampons
> Ajax: *a white tornado,* the Iliad, *stronger than dirt*
> Pine Sol: *And you are certainly not the pine-scented air. / There is just no way that you are the pine-scented air.*
> *If it's gotta be clean . . . It's gotta be* Tide

Where did my mother come from? She aimed, fired: *Buy a new seat. And nicer friends.* I tried an SOS-prayer to the heavenly call center staffed with angels and saints. *Let this seat come clean. Let me one day have hot bionic monkey sex and still remain a lady.*

My mother's voice found the towel Marla had used on her hands. It resembled the drapery in Gentileschi's *Judith Slaying Holofernes.* Curiously similar, only without the beheading, a fate I thought fit for Marla's one-night stand. In art class, I never supposed that mousy Sister Eleanor, who taught only female artists—plus O'Keeffe with no mention of vaginas—might be a subversive. After all, from the lunchroom, you could see her hang the nuns' panties on the clothesline, each pair billowing like a teensy spinnaker sail. And not one bra among them.

Swallowing It

How could my father have done it?
Shoved his hand in Mom's blouse at dinners,
the popped button, exposed breast,
the lewd, flicking tongue—

He shoved his hand in Mom's blouse, dinners,
egged us children to laugh along,
the lewd, flicking tongue—
Under her A-line, he grabbed her vagina.

Egging us children to laugh along,
he jerked down her panties; she said *no.*
Under her A-line, he snatched her vagina.
Night after night, she told him *no.*

He jerked down her panties; she said *no.*
We kids wouldn't eat, stuttered, blinked—
Night after night, she told him *no,*
her white panties and bra, a surrender.

We kids wouldn't eat, stuttered, blinked—
Her nipples, buds, he pinched to hurt her,
her white panties and bra, a surrender,
the renegade moles on her bottom slapped.

Her nipples, buds, he pinched to hurt her,
wiped what he called bush on his napkin.
I noted the renegade moles on her bottom,
his handfuls of cunt, its other name.

He wiped what he called bush on his napkin.
She held the skillet close to his head.

I saw his handfuls of cunt, its name,
while she served him home-cooked meals.

She held the skillet close to his head,
said, *Put your napkins in your laps.*
She served her best, minding our manners.
Keep your elbows off the table.

ii.

Put your napkins in your laps.
I wanted the skillet to crack his skull.
Keep your elbows off the table.
I wanted the gravy to blister his face.

I wanted the skillet to crack his skull.
Your father's finished, clear his plate.
I wanted the gravy to blister his face.
Get up, do it now, she said.

Your father's finished, clear his plate.
Her first would be a smack to my mouth.
Get up now, I said do it.
The next would be a charley horse.

Her first, a smack to my mouth—
Dad's laugh, her privates bared.
The next, she'd give a charley horse.
She'd lift me by the hair, I'd refuse.

Dad's laugh, her privates bared—
no steel wool between *my* thighs.
She'd lift me by the hair, I'd refuse:
Hit me again, I won't clear his plate.

No steel wool between *my* thighs,
my father sucking food from his teeth,

I'd say, *Go ahead, hit me again.*
She'd bang my head against the wall.

My father sucking food from his teeth.
The popped button, exposed breast—
She bangs my head on the wall.
I say, No.

The Promised Land

Mom loaded us in the backseat of her Fury. Leaving Dad. For good. The car followed familiar turns to Grandmom's house in a wealthier suburb. Our promised land, our finest hour. Life was as good as the red apple I munched.

At the last cocktail party, Mom stood by her sumptuous spread—flawless china, French, gilded with eighteen-carat flowers; silver accoutrements; crystal goblets; and a starched white tablecloth she'd cross-stitched herself. Dad threw the first punch that her new dress hid her *bitty titties* and showed her *cottage-cheese legs*. He waved a set of swizzle sticks of naked African women whose hair he called *nappy*, teeth *bucked*, breasts *saggy like jigaboo Zulus*, droopy enough to perch on the glass's rim so the stick wouldn't fall in the whiskey. *Is that what you're wearing?* he mocked. *You look like Mother Mary, a Vestal Virgin, and God knows I don't get any ass from you.* Clasping his hands, he rolled his eyes skyward, praying in tongues. From behind the pink brocade sofa, I watched the face behind Mom's face melt like candle wax. The fake face she wore for guests scanned the room, saw their belly laughs, and laughed her humiliation along with them. Little, I couldn't break those swizzle sticks and stab them in his eyes. I couldn't take his highball glass and smash it on his teeth.

Finally, we were leaving him, we'd be free, happy, without fear—until Mom veered into my podiatrist's driveway, slowly turned the car back, and said, *No, we're Catholic, she'll say go home, work it out.*

Mastering Culinary Arts

You don't cook. Her utensils hard-pressed you,
rolling pin smacking your back, hot spatula held
to your eye, knee driven in your thigh for refusing.

You wouldn't serve them. Training to be male,
you were fierce fists until the day you failed
to fit your hips in straight-cut boy jeans.

You learned the art of starving, hours of running,
eating only what your mother could force blow
by blow. Razor thin, you cut, *I won't be you.*

When the sixth doc said, *You can't be too rich or too thin,*
you rolled your eyes, gained ten pounds on ice cream.
By 95 you could survive, though it would take years to live.

Burden of Proof

The day my father breaks my nose, I fly
down Guernsey Avenue, then up Cumberland Road,
swallowing blood between breaths.

When I creep home, he tries
to beat me again, chases me close,
fists swiping air, overturning chairs.

Cornered in the bathroom with a boning knife
squeezed in my hand, I taste blood like a blade,
as if that weapon had rusted in my mouth.

A clean thrust to the throat, I think,
should work, then jerk the blade to gut him.
But my brother's shrieks cut through my haze,

his toothpick body sticking in the door frame,
a chalkline holding Dad at bay until the den door bangs
and, as if it were a movie, in walks Mom.

Dad leaves on a fetid wind. *Help,* my only word
before her tongue stings me back in place,
How dare you ruin my day?

Sunday Night Dinners

I miss my grandmother's hands. Small and delicate,
smooth with fragrant lotion. Rice paper skin, blue veins,
translucent pink polish; she was a watercolor.

All that she touched seemed softer. In her hands,
the cast-iron skillet seemed soft, the china and silver
set for dinner, soft, her highball glasses of whiskey, soft.

After dinner, she sat in the rocking chair, listening to me
play guitar, badly. Her wits softer from the drink,
the shine from her diamonds in the half-light, soft,

her hands clapping with enthusiasm, spreading the scent
of lavender and milk, while she'd catch the tuneless
coming toward her and toss back nothing but song.

III

Reworkings: Stieglitz's Photo of O'Keeffe Painting a Watercolor

i.

Annoyed by his disruption, she emerges from her painting,
a white flower in dense leaves, and locks her eyes on the distance

to protect a secret, stone rough in the hand. How
can we see origins, the self eclipsed by fear's laughter

nixing a boy's shy kiss, rainfall ending a home-run play, loyalty
earning a first detention, the priest trying to enter me by force?

I'd have climbed inside O'Keeffe's flower if the petals had opened,
if the stamens were grasses that could hide small animals.

ii.

In the photo, my lips smile wide, not my eyes. He beams, hugs
me vise-tight, the white tab at his collar like the Eucharist,

his miraculous medal cold on my ear, the camera a portal through
which to view my hands practiced in braiding long, glossy hair,

knot palm leaves into flowers. Was O'Keeffe obsessed
with flowers, or was she caught off guard, scoffing,

*I hate flowers. I paint them because they're cheaper than models
and they don't move*—a pragmatic remark, but is it a lie

or a secret she works like the stone I turn, resurrect, can't let be.
The subject in the photo won't look at us, isn't about to tell.

How to Lose the Self

Let it fester.

Blow at it softly as you would a wishing weed.

Watch each floret drift on humid air.

Do not collect them or try to press them back into a flower.

Whatever you do, do not breathe in.

I have heard if you let the spirit leave, something else will dwell there.

If this is true, don't drown.

Open your eyes to the murk.

Don't fight. Nor raise a hand as if to refuse a second helping.

At the beach, let them kick down your castle.

Let mice run crazy in the maze of your head.

Suppress rage like a ball submerged in water.

Launch the ball. You might break free.

The Art of Shape

Neither Rubens' nude, nor Degas' dancer,
maybe Ingres' *La Grande Odalisque*—
I don't care if I'm no longer svelte,
buffed, rawboned, starved.

Cadaverous, ethereal—I don't care
if I'm no hot-hipped head turner,
no longer built to dance, all legs,
muscled, sculpted, daddy longs, gone.

Sick of years of counting calories,
even toothpaste, mornings, nights,
though never one to choke half-chewed food,
kneel before the bowl, eyes fixed on

the deodorant bar, hands gripping the seat
like a life ring. No, I was disciplined as a nun,
rigid, clavicle and rib, hips
mere bone, curves hard as stone,

cocky at 100 then 90 then less,
judging bulimics as weak barbarians
who'd ruin their pearly whites
while mine shone perfect. And so,

I don't care, headache and exercise just too draining,
the silly doctor's reverse psychology—
You can't be too rich or too thin—
stupid, yet somehow smart to him.

When I looked in the mirror, I'd see
Botero's *Bath,* not images
in photos that never lied:
gaunt cheekbones you'd see in a Schiele,

a frightened woman, lean as a snake,
hard as brick, perfectly manicured.
Now, my body's 30 pounds overweight, my heart
nourished by my spongy belly, dimpled thighs,

the little jiggle around my middle—
by my courage to love this shape, full and new.

My Fist That Punched the Window

I removed the sutures too soon,
let them pucker into keloid

lumps, poked them to find
fragments of *oh* and *yes,*

like relics awakening,
welcome as winter sun.

Glass, blood, and pain
came out of the wound.

What had seeped *in*
was the pulse

of my voice—poised
to escape into song.

My Father's Heart

Four score and seven beers ago,
my father scoffed at the Liberty Bell
the day we toured Philadelphia: first flag,
art museum, Franklin Institute's walk-through heart.

Down the walls of its atriums, I slid,
stuck my arms into pulmonary veins,
played Venus flytrap with valves,
woo-wooed in the vena cava.

The smooth walk-through heart thumped,
glug-glugging like a drowning timpani.
That heart was a healthy rose, the valves
big enough to stick my head in.

Years later, Dad's heart balked in its socket,
the EKG glowing like a radar screen,
lights blinking like fireflies I would catch
and jar on summer nights.

He trembled under the snowflake gown,
as if beneath new powder, and I was moved
to witness his pain, the brute I knew
restrained by wires little thicker than hair.

He snarled, *Get off the fucking call button,*
or I'll cut your fucking hand off.
My father refused the call button
as fierce as the host at church—

No succor from God or the nurse,
no extra pills in a hospital cup, no pharos
glow of the firefly's tail, nor moment
of flight before the flutter stopped.

My Mother's Chores

On hands and knees,
scrubbing the floor,
the kettle's shriek
sends her
rushing
to the burner.
I hear the suck
of water
draining
before she dashes
dough with flour,
presses, patty-cake,
with heels of hands,
a crust for
apple pie.
When her hearing aids are in,
she answers the phone,
chats with convivial
desperation—
He never thanks me,
her voice a ship
lifting in a stormy sea.
Sweet-smelling stew
seethes in the pot.

The Little Engine That Could

How you'd rage for my mouth
or any soft place you could strike hard enough
to knock me across the backseat of that Fury,
but I refused to learn, to behave, my soul
dying of thirst, like a plant you forgot to bring back.
You hated being mother and father,
so you hit more, knocked the *say-cheese* smile
off my face for photos, smacked me again
for not smiling. There'd be no wasting
the work you put into starched dresses,
patent leather Mary Janes, white gloves, holiday hats—
and, later, when my wounds started showing—
depression, deliberate overdose—you dressed them
with money, the only way you knew to help.
You'd press furtive cash in my palm
with the remorse of a relapsed addict,
leave me to friends, professionals—to anyone
who could, who would save the girl you loved.

My Wound

My wound is delinquent, impudent; carries
A barefaced chain that would hold you hostage
Coils its fists, skin on fire, consumed entire to char

My wound hurls rocks at the faultless wall
Lays its fevered head on your breasts
Tears inking your body

My wound is the beak of a baby robin, neck straining for worms
My wound is a canyon where a climber falls to untimely death
My wound, like my sex, is hungry

With its mouth that opens and shuts
Hinged, my wound will not stay closed
It's the broken window and hand that smashed it

Printing press and conveyor belt
My wound sends news all over town
Its envelope's sealed, then slit open

It's a hymen broken for a life of touching
Its coyotes rip a fresh kill
It's an oyster with black pearls in its mouth

My wound is out of breath, a chrysalis exhaling its butterfly
It's a tunnel, an exit, an off-ramp
Busts the windshield, bloodies the bat

At night, my wound flies through the cosmos
Burning holes in sky's dark skin
By day, my wound walks, sun burning its shoulders

My wound is selfish, would swallow you whole
Break into your house at night
Curl like a cub at the foot of your bed

My wound says *fuck you* and *please love me*
It won't heal but for your hands, your voice
When my wound stops retching

And you, who have no fear
Intrepid, you fight, no nunchucks or gun
Give empty hands that take mine

Give empty arms that hold me
My wound leads to nowhere, to all
But for you, it suddenly quakes with thanks

Watching Her Neigh

If I paint a wild horse, you might not see the horse . . .
but surely you will see the wildness! —Pablo Picasso

Rear and crash, rear and crash—her fists slam down on the
hood of his Mustang. *You promised me, you promised,* she
sobs, pounding the '66 classic, light blue.

She howls, *You lying cheater,* his face stunned as if tasered,
blush zesty for bystanders. She growls and heaves a rusty
bike on the white ragtop, ripping it.

Clearly on behalf of the Mustang, a groan from a
male onlooker: *That restoration'll cost big bucks.* No
one intervenes.

The young man bear hugs her and they spin and she bites
him and tries to break free. He lets her go, springs in his car,
and drives off, tires skid-marking pavement.

Someone says, *Piss and vinegar.* Someone else says, *That
car's fucked.* And I think of material costs for restoration:
wrenches, screws, glues, pliers, polish, paint. I've spent years
reinventing, and the best I could make of me is an abstract
Picasso:

feet where eyes should be, sex where mind should be, all
elbows and knees, deformed, disfigured, warped. Where I'd
liked to have been his *Woman in White,* I became the model
in *Ne Se Tordant les Chevaux:*

triangular-based pyramids for legs, spherical rear and breasts, cuboid neck, axis waist, and an oval-shaped face tipped skyward, hands fixing my hair.

Oh, my body! Balanced strong and wild on those legs, intact, peaceful, having stampeded the blue pigment from my heart, pain draining as slowly as paint strained through paper, through a sieve, like water wrung gently from my long, dark curls.

IV

Last Things

Before he was bedridden and had to wear adult
diapers, my dad wanted only to stand while he peed.
My brother and I would take him under the arms
and, on the count of three, hoist his big bear's body
from the recliner that had become his bed.
We helped him shuffle to the bathroom,
my brother bearing more of the load
as I pushed Dad's legs forward with my thigh.
A couple of times, I pretended that instead of hanging on,
my dad hugged me, saying *Atta girl, you've done well.*
But really, he was moaning, pained.
By the time we reached the toilet, he'd be out
of breath, confused, too sick for his modesty.
My brother and I knew the gift we gave Dad
each time we did this, and even when he lost aim,
and I didn't have the heart to hold his penis
like a parent might a distracted toddler's,
and he peed down my leg, I didn't mind:
he had to need us then, which felt something like love.

Nothing Left to Brace Against

After hours wondering
whether Dad would die
from morphine
or drown in his own fluids, I slept,
rooting for the morphine
to take him to the Savior
he believed in. When I rose,
looked at his lifeless face,
frozen that way, as Mom would
threaten, in absolute horror,
the tyrant was gone.
No regret. No hope.
His fair skin, my skin.
His dark hair, my hair.
His long legs, my legs.
The shape of his face, hands—mine.
The ice blue eyes of my life's love
terror-locked as once was I
on a distant corner.

My Father's Wallet

While he could still sit up and before dying,
my father hid his wallet from my mother.

He called her *spendthrift*, a critic's blame unchanged,
even as he strove to swallow water and make it to the john.

His stingy finally funny, we made bets
on where he'd stashed that billfold, its worn,

black leather curved to the sag of his rear,
padded by presidential faces rubbed soft.

The vicious money battles between millionaire's
daughter and trolley driver's son were nothing short

of epic. If he could have, he would have kept her reined
into the afterlife, so when the coroner needed an ID,

we searched the drawers within his reach,
and like the dog's poorly hidden bone,

the wallet was buried in the recliner, beneath the cushion
where his last breath wheezed.

Self-portrait as a Perspective Drawing

Where exactly was the vanishing point in childhood?
Which was the specific day, which the specific hour?
I was erased in the time it might take a Disney
cartoonist to gum away Donald's legs.

X marked the gash in my palm,
X, the stigmata of the ashes of promise,
X, the tracks of a train that seemed to merge
to what appeared as one rail,
which disappeared.

X, the damning double chromosomes,
the support beams that propped
the house I'd have sworn
would blow to smithereens:

There was a roof and a beach scene
by our summer bungalow.
The horizon over the steel
blue water was always moving.
Away. Escape was forever slipping
beyond the prow of my father's boat.

There are perspectives beyond perspectives—
the vanishing point, the X we can see,
giving way to a reverse perspective:
the train tracks widening,
opening out to a field of poppies
whose red become more vibrant,
more distinct, defying
da Vinci's advice that *objects*
ought to be finished less carefully
the farther away they are.

What if forever grew more vivid, not pale,
if my former life were to shed
like a night snake's patterned
skin, gray husk left to dry
in mountain sun, freed brilliance—

a calm past, a future joyride for the journey.
Nothing can stand in my way,
since from nothing comes all, new vanishing points,
X after X for our imperfect world.

The Repair

When my front tooth fell
in the birthday Guinness,
and I watched it sink
like an autumn leaf,
slow-motion through froth,
I did not worry
about the cosmos or mortality
but of the cosmetic mess.

I spooned the tooth
from the pint's bottom
and tried to fit it,
clandestine, back in place.

Dead teeth from a bike accident,
braces as a tween, new teen
incisors, root canals, half caps,
grind guards, whitening—
Damn, it's expensive to age.

But to get here, how dear,
and grateful, I wouldn't go back.
I have a lovely new tooth in a smile
that hasn't been faked in years,
offered freely with my story,
my brimming froth of love.

Nakedness

(after Ellen Bass)

Still, I loved until dumbstruck,
clothes crumpled beneath me,
silk and denim grown abstract,
buttons and socks, sublime.

He made me the catch in a breath,
like the time I heard that animal
snarl in a thicket of yellow leaves,
the warning meant for me.

He made me forget how
the clergyman had splayed me,
miraculous medal cold at my ear,
chew crusted in his lips' corners.

Forget those parties, when my mouth
moved like a hand puppet's,
where I showed off, transformed
shame's blush to whiskey's bold note.

And when my father's dead eyes
were fixed in terror, as if
his necessary death-song
became the thunder of church bells,

this man soothed that leaving,
as well as others whose bags I'd packed, leaving
empty halves in the house: medicine chest,
closet, dent on one side of the bed,

where I had rolled, fallen in the shape
of heartache. How grateful

I am to stand and take
my place among the vulnerable.

Grieving

(for S. H.)

First, I speed to Sukki's house. Allow her to crowd her table
with treats: Zinfandel, cheeses, chocolates, nuts. Nothing
too extravagant for my sorrow. Girlfriend's so generous, I
half expect her to sever her fern's frond to cool the heat of
my sobbing. Women bloom in nurture, our petals open like
arms to grief.

Later, go to Jack's house. Greedy, I want my body consoled.
Go past his wish to be invisible to tears, beyond his
armadillo reluctance, to the compassion softening the
chiseled cuts in his face. Be grateful for his silence as we
rock. Let sorrow depart, let it leave—to the place where the
final shudder goes once it has left the body.

Please

(after Jericho Brown)

stroke my hair like you'd touch suede, let water
fall through your curled fingers, trace your nails
through a zen garden, press moss around a rose bush.

stroke my hair like you'd peel avocados, smooth
wrinkles from the arm of a blouse, untangle twinkling
christmas lights, rinse suds from under your rings,

like you'd smudge charcoal to blend an image,
soften tangles with a round brush, sweep crumbs
from a bread knife, fluff a down pillow for sleep.

stroke my hair like you'd cradle a teacup, brush an eyelash
off your cheek, like you'd ease tissue from a gift,
feel your way through the midnight house, knowing.

Notes

"My Father the Bard": "Eleanor of Abington," a pun on Eleanor of Aquitaine, refers to my mother and the suburb we lived in, Abington, Pennsylvania. "Droich-chaint" is Irish for "bad words."

"My Father's Animals": *El Señor Bing* is a 1961 album by Bing Crosby.

"Forbidden Fruit": *The Apple Dumpling Gang* is a 1975 Disney film. *Jaws* is a 1975 American horror/thriller film directed by Steven Spielberg and based on Peter Benchley's novel.

"Call Center for Madonna/Whore Support": *St. Catherine Exorcising the Demon from a Possessed Woman* is a seventeenth-century engraving by an artist in the French School. "And you are certainly not the pine-scented air. / There is just no way that you are the pine-scented air" is respectfully borrowed from Billy Collins' poem "Litany." Artemisia Gentileschi's *Judith Slaying Holofernes* is held in the Uffizi Gallery in Florence.

"Mastering Culinary Arts" and "The Art of Shape": It is said that Wallis Simpson coined the phrase "You can't be too rich or too thin."

"Reworkings: Stieglitz's Photo of O'Keeffe Painting a Watercolor": The photo is one Stieglitz's took of O'Keeffe at Lake George, 1918.

"The Art of Shape": Ingres' *La Grand Odalisque* is held in the Louvre. Fernando Botero is a Colombian figurative artist. Egon Schiele was an Austrian painter and major figurative painter of the early twentieth century.

"The Little Engine That Could": This is the title of a classic children's book by Watty Piper, with the well-known line "I think I can! I think I can!"

"Watching her Neigh": *Ne Se Tordant les Chevaux* is a work by Pablo Picasso.

"Nakedness": The title of this poem is respectfully borrowed from Ellen Bass.

"The Repair": Guinness, a damned good Irish dry stout, originated at St. James' Gate, Dublin.

"Please": The title of this poem is respectfully borrowed from Jericho Brown. The Zen garden to which I'm referring is a small, tabletop version.

About the Author

Lindsey Royce received her Ph.D. in Creative Writing and Literature from the University of Houston. She also holds an M.A. from New York University and an M.F.A. from Brooklyn College. Her poems have appeared in numerous journals, including *Cutthroat, Empty Sink Publishing, Mudfish, New York Quarterly, Poet Lore,* and *Washington Square Review.* The recipient of a Cambor fellowship, along with several residency awards, Royce is currently Professor of English at Colorado Mountain College in Steamboat Springs, Colorado where she teaches writing and literature courses, including creative writing.

Made in the USA
Middletown, DE
06 October 2016